KU-547-195

A Pocket Guide to Defining Entrepreneurs

Maxwell Saban

For the Aquarius in us all

Introduction

Entrepreneurship can mean different things to different people. Academically speaking the definition is wide and far from straightforward. If someone were to ask me what an entrepreneur is or does, I would say that the focus lies on the individual being able to undertake one or more business opportunities in pursuit of profit. They should be able to recognise opportunities that others cannot. It is not simply about being a businessperson, it is about looking for gaps in the market and exploiting these gaps for profit. The risk-taking propensity of the individual is high, and their thirst for opening and retiring business opportunities and taking on new ideas is also a major driver for entrepreneurs.

If you imagine the Dragon's in Dragons Den (a television programme featuring entrepreneurs pitching to prospective "Dragon" investors), the Dragon's will invest in various business opportunities. They will hold on to some of their bigger businesses for a long time but, when it comes to new ideas, they may look to exit a short time after they've received an acceptable return on their investment. What's more, some of these Dragon-type entrepreneurial investors only wish to participate in businesses that are at a certain stage of development. This is because experienced entrepreneurs recognise what they are good at and what they are not so good at. If you can do this and/or surround yourself with people who can pick-up on your shortcomings, then an entrepreneur will increase their chances of success. Imagine being the smartest person in a room. What next? Should you stay alone or should you seek to surround yourself with smarter people?

This pocket guide provides an overview of the academic information available on entrepreneurship and gives the reader an insight into the entrepreneurial mind. It's helpful, because many of us desire this lifestyle or crave to understand how to achieve such success. It explores the elements of character, determination, and drive required to succeed.

However, from an entrepreneurial perspective, the path is not problem-free. You must be willing to accept that there will likely be highs and lows in business undertakings. It is not plain sailing to achieve success. To be successful, you will need to remain determined when pursuing your entrepreneurial ambitions.

Lastly, in my own undertakings it is necessary to make money work for you. This includes ensuring cash liquidity, access to credit, and investment as and when required. Credit is important for purchases, but liquidity is essential for survival.

In my own undertakings, I have had varied success, but one of the reasons I am publishing this work is to evangelise the importance of focus in achieving your goals.

Sometimes, whilst undertaking entrepreneurial pursuits, my focus has drifted as life has placed important events in my path and, thereby, distracted me from my business activities.

It requires a great deal of effort to pursue entrepreneurial exploits. If you're attempting to make extra cash, such as with a "side hustle" on top of a day job, then I applaud you. But, for every extra £1 you make outside of your normal profession, it's likely to require 3 times more effort.

Sometimes this can be the only option, as leaving a regular income for something new can sometimes be too big a risk, especially for new entrepreneurs. But, it's not unusual for the bigger risk to reflect a bigger opportunity, and higher financial gains.

Sir Alan Sugar recalls the time he purchased the football club Tottenham Hotspur as being one of the biggest distractions from Amstrad (his computer company). He believes had he applied full focus on Amstrad then it would have been far more successful had he not purchased the football club (Moreton, 2010).

Finally, I hope this guide provides you with a greater understanding of the characteristics required to become an entrepreneur. However, it is worth remembering that, as the world continues to change and develop, so too does the definition of an entrepreneur. And, no matter how the entrepreneur may be formally defined, the credentials and experience of an individual may also provide them with the legitimacy or credibility to warrant being called an entrepreneur.

Traditional views of the entrepreneur

Cantillon

The Irish economist Richard Cantillon first defined an entrepreneur as an individual who embraces a new business venture or activity, taking on some responsibility for its operation (Tan & Landrum, 2010), the founder of a new business or where a business didn't exist before (Gartner, 1985). Others believe that it's an innovative nature that defines an entrepreneur, by how they develop new ideas (Schumpeter, 1934). Furthermore, exploiting an opportunity may be regarded as entrepreneurial, such as discovering a gap in the market for a product or service (Peterson, 1985; Garfield, 1986).

The concept of entrepreneurship as 'exploitation' has changed, with original thoughts identifying profit as an exploitation of the working class (Knight, 1921). Moreover, it's the innovative approach that is the main element of what differentiates regular enterprises from an entrepreneurial enterprise. Above creating a new product or potentially a new enterprise, the entrepreneur is ultimately creating something unique and, in some cases, entrepreneurship is not isolated to small enterprises or even enterprise as traditionally defined in the corporate world (Drucker, 2007), as we will see below when discussing intrapreneurship in the 'Schools of Thought' chapters.

Aside from Cantillon's (1755) general definition of the entrepreneur, his own personal experience provided examples of the traditional tasks entrepreneurs undertook. Coming from an investment background, Cantillon's perspective is that an entrepreneurial activity or person should accept an element of risk (Cantillon, 1755).

Cantillon (1755) also notes that an entrepreneur is regarded as an intermediary between two other parties, and that the entrepreneur is the transformer (Cantillon, 1755). Gross (1884) illustrates this in his studies of two markets in which entrepreneurs take raw products or service provisions and turn them into finished goods, collecting profit throughout the transformation.

Say

Another great pioneer of the entrepreneurial definition is Jean-Baptiste Say (1815), whose work provides a link with more recent thinking on entrepreneurship. Say (1815) wrote from the viewpoint of the individual who educates others in shaping them to be ready for entrepreneurial tasks or activities. Say's (1815) focus was on understanding the importance of entrepreneurial activity and its concomitant importance on economic development. Say regards entrepreneurs as individuals with the potential to innovate (Filion, 2011). He sees entrepreneurs as practising innovation by creating more with fewer resources and having the ability to generate new ideas or ways of thinking through existing thoughts and, ultimately, "adding value" (Say, 1815).

Schumpeter

Another influential pioneer in entrepreneurship is Joseph Alois Schumpeter (1934) who provides a strong industry link through defining the link between innovation and entrepreneurs. He takes Say's definition and attempts to recognise the innovative links between entrepreneurs and their opportunities to engage in new ideas or activity.

Schumpeter introduces five concepts related to innovation:

1. The introduction of new goods
2. The introduction of new methods of production
3. The opening of a new market
4. The conquest of a new source of supply of raw material
5. The carrying out of a new organisation in any industry

(Schumpeter, 1934).

Schumpeter does, however, avoid addressing the issue of new venture development. Indeed, a problem with all three of the definitions of entrepreneurship cited above is that they are based solely on subjective analysis. They use a small sample to seek an understanding of the nature and the definition of entrepreneurship, with much of their analysis based on the direct, subjective observations of Cantillon, Say, and Schumpeter. Whilst their definitions have been used as an academic foundation, their contribution may ultimately be a simplistic representation of the complex nature of the modern entrepreneur (Filion, 2011).

Modern views of the entrepreneur

Aitken

In reaching a definition, Aitken (1963) makes an important distinction in defining entrepreneurs and understanding the nature of entrepreneurship. He says in looking for characteristics that define an individual as being an entrepreneur, these characteristics are made purely by association to the firm or project that is undertaken. The entrepreneur is an entrepreneur by association to the venture or project that is entrepreneurial. Assessing an individual for entrepreneurial-like behaviour may only be beneficial when reflecting on an entrepreneurial undertaking and, vice versa, when assessing a perceived entrepreneurial venture (Aitken,1963).

However, reaching a definition of entrepreneurship can only be made by first looking at the entrepreneur to see what themes are demonstrated. There is a causal relationship between the actions and the outcomes (Fayolle, 2007). To combat this,

Dana (1995) simply defines entrepreneurship as the ongoing business activity of the entrepreneur.

Gartner

Gartner (1990) identifies eight major themes in his definition. Within the theme there is an understanding of the entrepreneur and entrepreneurship:

1. Entrepreneurship is about the individual entrepreneur demonstrating certain characteristics
2. There is a link to innovation
3. It is implied that a new project or venture will suffice
4. There is a creation of value
5. Some researchers limit entrepreneurship to the private sector, others extend it to the public sector
6. Entrepreneurship is of importance to high growth organisations
7. Entrepreneurship involves something unique
8. Entrepreneurship is connected to owning/managing

Defining the entrepreneur is tackled in a variety of ways. Whilst there may be underlying themes throughout much of the literature, Stevenson and Gumpert (1965) note that not having a skill in a defined entrepreneurial area does not necessarily mean an entrepreneur is less entrepreneurial. They discount the view that the entrepreneur has an "all or nothing" set of personality traits. When referring to taking on entrepreneurial ventures or projects, one extreme may be the 'promoter type' of entrepreneur who feels confident in seizing all opportunities and is confident in their ability. The other end of the spectrum may be the trustee who feels threatened by change. They are more likely to utilise resources based on predictability rather than opportunity for success. Entrepreneurs are likely to lie between these two extreme viewpoints (Stevenson and Gumpert, 1985).

Factors that define the entrepreneur

There are a great number of definitions that look at entrepreneurs from a variety of viewpoints. Moreover, some definitions call for several different viewpoints to categorise the entrepreneur as being 'entrepreneur-like' (Julien, 1998). Fillion (2011) summarises the key entrepreneurial traits identified in the literature that seeks to define entrepreneurs.

Innovation

As discussed previously, according to Schumpeter, (1947), the definitive definition of an entrepreneur is related to the innovative process conducted, it is about doing something new or taking something old and adding a new concept, edition or adaptation. Changes in the economic aspects of society centre on entrepreneurial activity. Adaptive responses in society to economic issues are often about taking what exists before and attempting to offer solutions based on resources already available. Whilst creative responses attempt to provide a new idea or thought to a previous economic issue, possibly changing or shaping economic structure differently for the future. This in effect provides a solution or bridges gaps where a provision may have been absent before (Schumpeter, 1947).

Drucker (2007) identifies, above all, entrepreneurial management as the systematic need for innovation, to discover and exploit new opportunities to fulfil a human need. Innovation can be regarded as a key tool for entrepreneurs, allowing them to take advantage of change, creating new businesses and enterprises. To initiate innovative thinking successfully, entrepreneurs need to understand the principles of how to apply innovation. Entrepreneurship with its perceived high-risk factors, particularly in highly innovative sectors such as micro computing, have high failure rates in ventures. This is often because entrepreneurial resources are given to a venture where high innovation already exists in a market sector already. Despite this, companies such as 3M have demonstrated high innovation through low risk, with four out of five new inventions being successful.

Entrepreneurship and innovation should be considered an integral part of society for the sustainment of life in organisations and the economy. From a social standing, Drucker (2007) believes that innovation through entrepreneurship is needed on a number of levels, to combat social unemployment and combat failing government policy. Whilst the benefit for the entrepreneur is that they continue to exploit opportunities and develop their skills.

In addition to understanding the entrepreneur as a risk taker (as discussed below) and having a desire to be successful, another personality dimension is their ability to transform ideas into reality, through invention or innovation of an existing product/service (Julien, 1989). Whilst the entrepreneur contributes to the formation of the economic system, their existence does not lend support to theories of equilibrium. Whilst in today's society, supply and demand can never be definitively predicted, the entrepreneur contributes to this endeavour. The entrepreneur seeks to tip any balance of equilibrium, with new projects or ideas, contradicting the ideas of economics through innovation, thereby having the potential to profit when the economy is in support of their idea, before refreshing and looking at something else (Julien, 1989). Leibenstein (2001) poses the view that if there was equilibrium in terms of competition, all inputs and outputs could be perfectly predicted, and there would be no need for entrepreneurship as the process of innovation and alike would be easy to establish. However, he adds that it is difficult to channel resources to meet these economic outputs and therefore this is what gives an entrepreneur their opportunity (Leibenstein, 2001).

SIR **JAMES**

Dyson, the worldwide super brand founded by James Dyson, had one motivation. "A lot of things don't work very well or there's something you don't like about it, and so we set about getting rid of that and, you know, other people aren't bothering to do that". This view is true, how many times have you picked something up and thought this could be a lot better. The Dyson vacuum cleaner is known as a device that never loses suction and, with this in mind, they've taken other ideas forward with the same mindset. However, before this vacuum cleaner was a success, Dyson produced 5,126 prototype failures before discovering the winning cleaner we now know so well (CBS, 2017).

However, with innovation comes advances that people need to know and understand.

"We're putting more and more technology into products which need explaining. People need to be able to tell the difference" Dyson said. "We're trying to break conventions. You think battery machines are useless, batteries fade. Ours don't. So we want people to be able to see that." At the heart of their technology and design", Dyson said, "is the idea of making things smaller and more efficient".

And, of course, as Dyson mentioned with reference to his earlier prototype, failing frequently and consistently is key to ongoing success. Speculative reports show that Dyson considered the development of the electric car as early as 1993 however, through a combination of borrowing parts from other manufacturers and not being an automotive specialist, this dream was just a step too far for the Dyson corporation in terms of commercial viability. Although this constraint didn't stop them developing multiple other innovations that are now consumed in both domestic and business markets (Dikes, 2022).

Risk

Cantillon's (2010) view is that the entrepreneur provides an important foundation for the whole economic system. He believes that the best market is a free market where entrepreneurs can make their own decisions on customer choice, trusting their own judgement of what will sell (Cantillon, 2010). This ideology mimics the work of Adam Smith's invisible hand in which he assumes that the free market will be sufficient, as if it were governed by regulation (Saucier, 2010). The risk associated with entrepreneurship, in Cantillon's view, is due to competition and changing interests in the consumer. Due to competitive environments, entrepreneurial incomes will vary significantly and, for the individual, bankruptcy is perhaps today's equivalent of a venture failing (Cantillon, 2010).

Knight (1921) reports that Say (1852) believes that profit is a reward for risk taking and that whilst profit might be compared with that of a capitalist building society (more and more profit building), the profit and risk relationship is more transferable to the entrepreneur. Furthermore, Knight (1921) adds that profit can be a reward for a change in perspective which may add risk that could contribute to enterprise failure. For entrepreneurs who take higher wages or create higher profit, this is seen as a reward for the perceived risk in entrepreneurial activities (Mangoldt,1855). However, receiving additional profit for additional risk, according to Gross (1884), is unsustainable as losses and gains in profit would eventually cancel themselves out. Mithoff (1885) adds that profit is not necessarily the reward for risk taking, but the wage that entrepreneurs receive may be a reward for operating a venture that has potential to fail rather than looking at just profit. In some cases where the entrepreneur is not the owner of the business, more the transformer, there is an element of risk removal whereby, if the entrepreneur has nothing to lose, he bears no risk (Mithoff, 1885). Hawley (1907) believes there is a strong link between the risk bearing of an entrepreneur and the reward in terms of profit they make. However, little is explained by the research that identifies a connection between risk and uncertainty. For example, the paradox of taking rewards for risks that are known is one position, while assuming reward for risks that are not identifiable is another (Knight, 1921). However, whilst uncertainty is in some way seen to be measurable in business through mathematical probability, the risk involved with entrepreneurial activity may be less measurable (Knight, 1921). The element of risk for entrepreneurs that cannot be insured against, gives rise to entrepreneurs that are fortunate in being successful, sometimes going against negative speculation and odds (Hawley, 1907). Moreover, if risks were to be measurable, then there would be no reward for risk taking, as these elements of profit would be factored in (Knight, 1921).

Palmer's (1971) view on defining the entrepreneur is that many previous frameworks define the entrepreneur through the measurement of functional behaviour. The idea is that an entrepreneur must demonstrate several different characteristics before they are regarded as an entrepreneur. However, these functional measurements are crucial to separate the non-entrepreneur and the entrepreneur (Smith, 1971).

Smith (1971) identifies that entrepreneurs with a 'need for achievement' are more willing to take on tasks where there is a form of risk involved (Smith, 1971). McClelland (1962) hypothesises that individuals with high achievement needs will be drawn to carrying out business tasks, as these tasks allow the entrepreneur to complement their thirst for achievement in risk taking and profit making. (McClelland, 1962).

Palmer concludes in his work that the entrepreneurial function is as much about risk taking as risk measurement. The entrepreneur should be able to assess a given risk within a venture and act accordingly to minimise that risk or maximise benefit from the opportunity. A successful entrepreneur would be one who could minimise the risk to the lowest level possible. Lastly, an individual's perception of risk could be inherent from beliefs that were created in childhood (Palmer, 1971).

Risk for an entrepreneur cannot just be determined by decision making. Many decisions businesses and executives make daily have a predetermined certain outcome (Belshaw 1955; McClelland, 1961). Carrying out mechanical or repetitive tasks have minimal risk. Risk taking for the entrepreneur should be about making decisions where the outcome may be relatively uncertain. However, risk again may be minimised by knowing facts or possessing information that indicates probable success (McClelland, 1961).

McClelland (1961) describes successful entrepreneurs as having n type achievement. This can be described using a child's ring toss game. Children who have little entrepreneurial achievement will stand relatively close to the target and try more often, whilst children with a higher level of n achievement will place themselves in a position that increases uncertainty. Their position enables them to have a chance to meet the target. Their position elicits moderate risk. They are not so close that they will definitely meet the target, but they are not so far as they will not stand a chance. They also receive a level of satisfaction if they are successful (McClelland, 1961).

SIR
RICHARD
BRANSON ON RISK

Sir Richard Branson believes the biggest risk you can take is investing in a business that you know nothing about. Whilst Virgin today seems to be a conglomerate of sorts, originally all of Virgin's ventures were linked to a core business proposition. Of course, as Branson's business ideas developed, so did the direction of his entrepreneurial activities. He recalls selling Virgin Records as being one of the biggest risks he has ever taken. They had just signed the Rolling Stones, and the offer for £1bn from EMI at the time would have been difficult to turn down. Virgin needed a cash injection to fight off a British Airways legal battle which, eventually, Virgin won (Branson, 2017).

When he launched Virgin Atlantic, a now very operable business model, the cost of the plane alone put huge pressures on the rest of the business and Branson had to lease the plane, and keep Virgin Atlantic as a separate entity, while he evaluated its longevity and performance. On one occasion, a bird flew into the engine of Virgin's first plane, so they had to use their cash reserves to purchase a new one! Branson believes that there will always be something ready and waiting to knock an entrepreneur off balance, but this risk can be offset by keeping a razor-sharp focus (Rhythmsystems, 2020).

One of the less fortunate launches and business strategies was 'Virgin Cola', which engaged in several stunts and campaigns aimed at taking on Coca-Cola, an already well known and enjoyed premier coke brand. Of course, Virgin Cola failed to succeed in its war against Coca-Cola, and Virgin Cola was discontinued in 2009 (Clifford, 2017).

Despite Branson's failures and successes, he believes, "If you allow the fear of failure to become a barrier, you're already putting roadblocks in your way...Entrepreneurs take risks by attempting to change the status quo" (Coleman, 2018).

Coordination and management of resources

Cole (1942) poses the question of whether or not the coordination of management tasks to exploit innovation is a catalyst for profit making and a major function of the entrepreneur. Exploiting resources that have remained undiscovered or have not been recognised as opportunities may be an example of entrepreneurship. This is opposed to managers in general who have taken advantage of generally recognised resources combined with the development of advancing business skill and knowledge.

Aitken's (1963) view on the entrepreneur's coordination ability may not seem calculated in terms of success. "To the extent that behaviour in a business firm is organised (formally or informally), to that extent we have entrepreneurship; to the extent it is disorganised, random or self-defeating, to that extent entrepreneurship is lacking" (Aitken, 1963).

This statement allows for the understanding that entrepreneurship may include aspects of the management function. It raises the idea that entrepreneurship, even in its quest for success, may be non-ordered and chaotic. Aitken (1963) believes that organisation in an entrepreneurial venture to promote growth will be ever changing and adaptive to cope with changing environments, remaining flexible to meet changing business demographics. Innovation in terms of the entrepreneurial view is deemed ongoing and irreversible due to its progressive nature. This means that entrepreneurs need to influence the venture to react to innovative culture changes, remaining open and adaptive (Aitken, 1963).

When looking at business growth and expansion, Belshaw (1955) points out that whilst an entrepreneur may have the ability to expand and grow a venture, a more effective use of existing resources may contribute to the same result. If resources are not being used effectively, or to their full capacity, then there is additional growth capability of a venture without the need to make additional capital investment. In other words, you should utilise resources that are available to you. A country where there is a surplus amount of labour available will not require a piece of machinery that can minimise the need for labour resource, as the labour resource is widely available. An entrepreneur can take advantage of surplus resources around them. Similarly, if there is a large amount of land available for an entrepreneurial task, there is no need to preserve it. Less land will make the available land scarce and, therefore, there will be an opportunity for an entrepreneur to make the land s/he has available more productive and efficient. For the entrepreneur to reach these efficiencies, they work towards having the required technical knowledge (Belshaw, 1955).

When innovating new products or services there is often a need or opportunity to adopt support operations. For example, the development of meat transportation and the rolling out of meat production could lead to vertical integration and expansion through packaging innovation, product innovation, expanding production in different kinds of meat, and similar product integrations. This could be achieved by production of complementary products. For example, egg and dairy products are possible through the expansion of the original meat distribution functions (Chandler 1990). An indirect focus here is on optimising the supply chain wherever possible to minimise waste in vital resources, all the way from raw products to final distribution (Womack & Jones, 1996).

By adapting operations, enterprises are capable of exploiting markets. By moving operations closer to potential markets entrepreneurs can reach the markets more effectively. When innovating there is often a strong need to develop support processes based around the innovation. For example, when the Singer Sewing Machine was on the rise, the company felt it necessary to redefine distribution channels, adopting Singer Sewing outlets for sales, service and after care. These proved as effective as external distributors acting on commission (Chandler, 1990).

Leibenstein (1968) believes that entrepreneurs can be defined using the production function. If an entrepreneur enters an underdeveloped market or a market that is developed but lacks the relevant resources, then it is the entrepreneur's objective to make up for these deficiencies in resources. For example, when building a machine for production that is not available from their home country or importation. For the individual to be a successful entrepreneur in their chosen market, they must fulfil themselves with the knowledge and capability to build the machine. Twinned with their ability to make up for market deficiency, they must also have the ability to bridge gaps in projects. For example, find funding where none existed before, seek new opportunities, innovate, and manage risk and so on, as discussed in this chapter. The entrepreneur however is not necessarily regarded as being present due to market shortfalls or gaps. They may also be present because they are fuelled by self-motivation and desire to lead and hold responsibility for his/her venture.

Another important factor of understanding the entrepreneur is that for them to be regarded as an entrepreneur, they may be regarded as 'input completing'. They may have the relevant skills in finance, marketing and distribution for example but, to be an entrepreneur, they will need to have the ability to complete all parts of the project to a sufficient standard (Leibenstein, 1968).

Economic development is partly stimulated by an increase in income per capita which, in turn, is driven by a population increasing production and efficiency. Coupled with an entrepreneur's ability to multitask, an input-completer stretches resources to drive development (Leibenstein, 1968). The time in which gap bridging and input completing takes place will vary greatly between entrepreneurs. This may be due to the level of project shortfalls. This type of activity is likely to be costly to the entrepreneur in terms of resources but possibly in monetary terms too. The success of these functions will depend on the entrepreneur's capacity as well as their motivations. Their social status may also play an important part in delivery, in terms of whether they can network with the right people who may be able to provide access to resources. Leibenstein (1968) discusses the opportunity cost to entrepreneurs. In doing so, he believes that an analysis of potential profit against the potential of losing opportunities and falling behind other firms is what prompts entrepreneurs to make correct timely decisions (Leibenstein, 1968). In understanding the entrepreneur's ability to compete input functions there is often scarcity. It is also important to remember that there may be excess supply for those entrepreneurs who have a higher skill set in one area. This excess may be redundant to the market as a whole (Leibenstein, 1968).

Entrepreneurship may be regarded as a main cause of economic growth and development. Across societies there is a belief that this is the reason that there are different levels of growth and development. This would mean those that do not have the necessary supply of entrepreneurs would fall behind those societies that have a high level of entrepreneurs keen to perform the entrepreneurial function.

Entrepreneurs are more likely to arise under a certain set of societal conditions where individuals show a level of psychological traits that allows or encourages them to be entrepreneurial. Growth and development is caused by the rise of entrepreneurs due to social and psychological factors. There is an alternate view that entrepreneurship does not act as the creator or facilitator of economic development and growth. However, entrepreneurship is a transmitter for economic causes. Entrepreneurship is more likely to occur where there are favourable economic conditions. These conditions motivate the individuals to maximise their position. If the conditions are not favourable the economic society in question will generate lower development and growth. Under this view entrepreneurship remains a dependent variable and the psychological traits of the entrepreneur alone counts for very little (Wilken, 1979).

Entrepreneurship requires people to have different views on the value of resources for two different reasons. Firstly, the probability of joint production when resources are involved is almost a certainty, as a number of resources are combined to form most products and services. The element of profitability is crucial to the entrepreneur. He or she will value the resources far differently than the original owner of the resources (Casson, 1982). The entrepreneur must not disclose his margin of profit on the resources, as the resource holder may increase the value of the resource, diminishing the entrepreneur's profit from the venture. There may be a differentiation in price as each party is not aware that if the resource were differently represented its value may be worth considerably more. Moreover, in one market, a resource may be overpriced, whilst in another market, under-priced. The resource is battling for equilibrium, and whilst the entrepreneur in his/her innovative sense can tip the balance of equilibrium, taking advantage of tactical resource purchasing will yield him/her a profit opportunity whilst allowing the resource to meet equilibrium again. Then the process will repeat itself (Schumpeter, 1934).

MARK CUBAN

On Resource Management

Mark Cuban hates meetings and loves family time. Most of his day consists of creating email threads and avoiding having meetings wherever possible. Emails provide him with a database or reference point where he can pick up the desired information that he needs wherever possible. The email list acts as his priority list and, if he gets stressed, he'll go and shoot a few hoops. Come evening, he'll try and spend as much time as possible with his family (Rollings, 2020).

Here Mark sees himself as the finite resource, his time is scarce, and he needs to spend it as wisely as possible. This touches upon a modern idea, which is the importance of mental health. For example, taking a break when he is stressed is important as a stressed mind just isn't productive, nor does he take for granted the time that is spent on family.

Of course, this doesn't work for everyone or, you might say, it can't work for anyone. But, in the modern coordination of resources, whether personal or not, it raises the question as to how more effective you could be as an entrepreneur with a good night's sleep, a clear mind, and structure in place that allows you to rest.

Sometimes, a perfect work-life balance isn't always possible but, as we understand more about how to be more effective humans, we can unlock attributes in our minds that enable us to do things more effectively.

Value creation

Say's (1803) theory of value is linked to utility, in those exchanges of 'things' that warrant value (Forget, 1999). Price is the measure of value, and value the measure of utility (Schumpeter 1954). When an individual buys a product he is merely exchanging this for another product. "One sacrifices one utility to acquire another". The view is that what the person is using as a utility to exchange will be worth less than the utility they are receiving. Man will not exchange unless he has something to gain. The other utility is worth more to him than the utility he is exchanging, thus creating value.

In terms of price for items, whenever quantity exceeds demand the price will likely fall. However, the value of an item in terms of price can be different for different parties. The quantity of fresh water on a mainland will warrant a low price, whilst fresh water on a ship at sea will cause a higher price. When the need for demand extends the quantity of production, there is no basis on which to set a price for the item in a reasonable fashion (Say, 1803). Entrepreneurs may exploit these situations in terms of price. Rivers and water that are useful have value. However, for them to have a price, it is unlikely it would ever be a price that individuals would pay, so price does not govern here.

Whilst there are numerous definitions of an entrepreneur, a noticeable theme amongst much research is that of venture creation (Gartner, 1990).

Innovations are believed to add value to organisations. Without added value they are just inventions. Innovation and rapid growth brought about by the actions of the entrepreneur are value creating processes. Moreover, the entrepreneur is a starter, initiator and coordinator of an object, who creates value (Fayolle, 2007).

Bruyat and Julien (2000) believe that in order to define entrepreneurship or, indeed, an entrepreneur it is necessary to define the individual and the environment centred on the project or venture. Their research explores the link between the entrepreneur and new value creation. An entrepreneur is responsible for creating new value. This value creation forms part of a process in which there is a project established, then the individual (creator) uses the project to shape and make themselves a successful entrepreneur. They will devote a large proportion of their life to their venture and it will help in building their entrepreneurial skill, and develop the principles and ethics they stand for. There is a reciprocal relationship where the entrepreneur will learn from the venture and the entrepreneur will develop the project. Market price is the indication of the value added, when concerned with the entrepreneur, the private market whereby the buying and selling of goods and services takes place (Bruyat & Julien, 2000). The idea of understanding what adds value in an entrepreneurial venture draws upon existing theory to understand whether the relationship the individual has with his venture or project is in fact entrepreneurial.

ROCKEFELLER'S

VALUE CREATION

John D. Rockefeller believed his sole purpose in life was to make as much money as possible and then use it wisely to make improvements to mankind. Rockefeller pioneered the idea that leadership needs to set priorities, take key lessons from data, and create an operating rhythm within an organisation.

He was a true Philanthropist, founding the Standard Oil Company and, during his time, he was one of the world's wealthiest men. He didn't stop at creating value through his oil company exploits. Rockefeller helped launch the field of biomedical research, funding scientific investigation that contributed to vaccines for meningitis and yellow fever. He was a pioneer for medical training standards in the US and built China's first real medical school (Mansor, 2017).

He did a lot more with his money, championing public sanitation, pushing for education without prejudice on sex, race, or creed. He founded the University of Chicago and so much more. He saw his status and access to money as a source for good, creating value from differential opportunities outside of oil (Philanthropy Roundtable, 2023).

He was clever with his business exploits. In the oil industry he was able to buy up all of his competitors within a 6 week period, and eventually placed his oil company into a strategic trust.

He was not admired by all, but is responsible for antitrust regulations, strengthening of unions and his charitable exploits are hugely noticeable.

Projective and visionary thinking

The key elements of entrepreneurship are innovation, taking risks in some form, and being independent in course of action. This is highlighted in the main body of literature concerning entrepreneurship (Longenecker & Schoen, 1975).

As previously discussed, there is some debate as to how entrepreneurs assess the risks involved with a projected venture. Whilst it may be a case of gambling for future success or taking an optimistic rather than pessimistic view of the future, an entrepreneur may take risky decisions based on what is important to them. The intangibility of a venture to outsiders may be understood more by the potential outcomes of a new innovation that, for example, may take time to develop. Entrepreneurs within organisations or as individuals are seen to be strategic thinkers. They have an ability to choose a direction whilst aiming to source new ideas and opportunities, decide the best course of action, controlling or manipulating resources, or searching for resources with the aim to promote success in all outcomes. The entrepreneur must ensure they have the skills to forward-plan projects, allowing time to allocate and source resources. Coupled with this, they need a given ability to motivate and inspire peers and stakeholders. It is important they share or understand their vision (Longenecker & Schoen, 1975).

Within the small to medium enterprise (SME) category of entrepreneurs there continues to be a debate as to who can be classed as an entrepreneur. Generally speaking, the levels of innovation and risk-taking differentiate the entrepreneur from the general shopkeeper for example, although this characteristic, according to Longenecker and Schoen (1975), is slightly harder to differentiate entrepreneurs, as shopkeepers can be independent in their decision making. Entrepreneurs have the ability to engage with the unknown and not need to carry out the same tasks that hold a high amount of certainty (McClelland, 1961).

Within large corporations, individuals who show entrepreneurial flair according to the three traits above are often confined within the walls of the corporation (Longenecker & Schoen, 1975,). Similarly, entrepreneurs who manage many employees, where an individual is viewed as a visionary, demonstrate high success capabilities particularly in industrial settings (Ely, Adams Lorenz & Young, 1917).

An entrepreneur's vision is seen to evolve as a project is undertaken, driven by the entrepreneur's relation capability. Vision is also driven by leadership, energy and the degree to which an entrepreneur is directed by his/her own values. Vision is about being able to understand a future point and the direction in which an entrepreneur wants a venture to take. Whilst few of the entrepreneurs studied by Filion (1991) appear to show truly great visions for their ventures, those who did proved to be more successful. They have planned out a number of possible scenarios of where their business could be, given certain outcomes. A vision will enable an entrepreneur to work, step by step, to achieve their desired end outcome. A sound vision has the potential to motivate and stimulate those working around an entrepreneur. The people around the entrepreneur form part of the first part of visionary thinking, the relations. These relations can become highly motivating and contribute to achieving a highly thought-through vision (Filion, 1991).

A vision is a reference for an entrepreneur to review what s/he is doing compared to where s/he wants to be. It is also used as a tool to integrate any team or workers around them into working towards the same cause. If a team is involved in the entrepreneurial venture the entrepreneur may become a visionary via his/her communication skills. Presenting a vision and reflecting on it with the team to build perhaps an even better vision than originally thought. Key relationships around the entrepreneur will enable a vision (perhaps a dream) to become a reality (Filion, 1991).

THE VISIONARY:
PAUL POLMAN

Paul Polman is the CEO of the huge multi conglomerate Unilever, which owns over 1,000 brands, and has been focussed on ensuring the business is more friendly to the planet. He implemented the sustainable living programme in 2010, aimed at creating ongoing societal impacts for future generations. The main aspirations of the whole business are to help improve the health and livelihoods of over one billion people by 2020 and cut the environmental impact of the business in half by 2030. Already 40% of the company's energy comes from green sources, and waste has reduced by 85%, with factory emissions down by 37% (New York Times, 2023).

Visionary and thought-provoking leadership can take many forms. In this example, Paul attempts to solve a real-world issue with a firm that is big enough to make a difference on a global scale.

Focus on action

Baty (1981) describes the need to focus on action. Most notably the need to meet targets. From the moment funding is raised and approved, an entrepreneur will need to meet targets that were laid out in their business plan, if such a plan has been produced. Failing to meet or negotiating targets may be possible in the early stages. However, doing this on a continuous basis may mean that financing may fall short of the needs of the firm as it tries to grow. Helping others in an entrepreneurial firm (such as employees) to plan their time, is crucial to ensure deadlines are met and maintained. As well as financing, missing deadlines may mean the loss of opportunities, through lack of competitive advantage. Not releasing products at the right time may have detrimental effects on a firm.

THE CHANGE MAKER:

ADAM BRAUN

Adam is a renowned change maker, and key American businessperson, philanthropist and blockbusting writer. He is a former founder and CEO of Pencils of Promise, which has contributed to building over 400 schools around the world. He uses a unique "for-purpose" approach and his organisation has raised over $75M to address global education. He is recognised on a global scale as a change advocate and has been asked to address the White House as a keynote speaker. He is big on understanding that the world and your place in it serves a unique purpose.

Leadership

Hornaday and Aboud (1971) find that, when comparing male business owners, those with entrepreneurial characteristics demonstrate a higher need for achievement and effective leadership. They also have a higher desire to be independent and avoid support.

In my own experience, co-founders or visionaries have often lacked the full capacity to run and manage the business on a day-to-day basis, nor do they really want to. Management tasks often take care of the operation, whilst entrepreneurial leadership figures can be left to focus on the bigger picture.

Of course, in practice you cannot always have the luxury of being just a leader or a manager. In the early stages of a venture, you will often wear multiple hats, especially if budgets are tight. Whilst your vision may be strong you will be a generalist of sorts in many areas. When opportunities arise for you to let someone else focus on the areas you are not good at, ensure you take the opportunity to shift these responsibilities.

ESTÉE LAUDER'S

LEADERSHIP STYLE

Estée Lauder was not a laid-back leader. She was focussed on training her employees to a high standard. She liked to know what her employees were doing but she wasn't necessarily a micro manager or democratic, she remained somewhere in between. She taught employees the importance of customer service and educated them in understanding how and why they should always keep the customer happy. She pioneered complimentary gift principles but, most importantly, as she had started from the ground up, she always knew how to motivate her employees. She had been in their shoes and knew what it was like to face issues similar to the ones they had faced. Marketing the business was so important to her, she knew how to build a winning, unrivalled brand so pushed for the highest standards in this area.

Dynamo of the economic system

Weber (1964) states that there are two ways of organising available resources. The first is the rational sense of dividing resources up where they are required. Alternatively, there may be a division of resources to purely exploit the opportunity of profit.

This view of resources relates strongly to the amount of money available for each activity and plays an important part in understanding the use of resources in any economic system. Highly established economic markets that favour the movement of money may also favour high profit seeking enterprises such as the entrepreneurial venture (Weber, 1964). Moreover McCelland (1961) describes a society with n levels of achievement are likely to influence and cultivate more energetic and lively entrepreneurs that in turn may contribute to economic development.

More encouragement of entrepreneurial ventures will also have positive economic effects (Stevenson and Gumpert, 1985; Longenecker & Schoen, 1975).

Weber (1965) does not consider any aspects of what drives the individual to be successful and is more concerned with the impact these kinds of enterprises have on the structure of an economic society (McCelland, 1961, p.205).

New firm creation is seen as a catalyst for the creation of products and services. SMEs are likely to have a more direct input into the local economy rather than a multinational corporation that delivers the same product or service. The most notable role of the new firm with regards to defining an entrepreneur is the perception of innovation from new firms. Technological advancement and innovation has led to an increase in economic growth.

Technological advancement has meant that products and services can be created using fewer resources which can be diverted to other areas of the company. Small firms in Silicon Valley play an important part in technological innovation and can grow rapidly. Whilst smaller firms are seen to budget less for research and development than larger firms, they produce more inventions for the amount spent on R&D and produce more inventions than larger companies.

This may be due to their ability and need to be more innovative, to grow in the market and their ability to take risks is symbolic of their entrepreneurial spirit, something that larger firms may regard as a waste of resources if the risk is too high. Whilst the small firm plays a good role in technological development it is important to remember that not all small firms wish to innovate. There may also be a causal relationship between small firms who think of the idea, and larger firms that implement it (Storey, 1982). Amazon has adopted a culture of failing forward, where failure needs to be embraced rather than punished. It's the idea of failing fast and moving on; if you know something is going to fail, do it in the shortest amount of time and with the least resources. Of course, if someone is not doing their job properly this is a different kind of failure. This is about recognising and pushing for new ideas and innovation that ultimately allows Amazon to be more successful with their ideas over time (Landerman, 2019).

The entrepreneur is recognised as playing an important part in economic society. Emphasis on this has been confirmed by research in output per worker in a labour force. Where innovation has taken place, this has increased efficiency per worker. For innovation to take place, entrepreneurs will be required to champion process changes to ensure innovation is adopted efficiently. Entrepreneurs should be taken into consideration in high growth economies where entrepreneurial talent has played a part in driving change and economic development. It would be wrong to ignore the entrepreneur's place in an economy, although important to remember an economy that promotes high growth may introduce training and development needs to create entrepreneurial talent. Because of the entrepreneur's role in economics to promote growth and prompt innovation development, those who are concerned with promoting growth will be keen to promote the supply of entrepreneurs to the given industry. Understanding what can stimulate and encourage the entrepreneur can contribute to economic growth (Baumol, 1968). Dubai with its lucrative tax benefits provides a stimulus for entrepreneurs. Many accelerators and agencies have been set up over the past 20 years across the UAE aimed at encouraging entrepreneurs and the formation of start-ups (Gov.ae, 2023).

Moffat (1976) defines the economic resources as land, labour and capital. Entrepreneurial ability is often added as a fourth economic resource. Entrepreneurial ability allows for the grouping of other resources through the process of management and risk taking, etc. This economic resource is considered less tangible than land, labour, and capital, as entrepreneurship is often combined with one or more to create production. An economy with entrepreneurial ability is said to be more productive than one that is not. Labour and entrepreneurial activity combined can be referred to as human resources and land and 'capital non-human resources'. Some believe it is not entrepreneurship but just good management that increases production (Moffat, 1976).

DAVID &
SIMON REUBEN

The Reuben brothers are two of the UK's wealthiest entrepreneurs. They were born in Mumbai in British India, before moving to the UK. They originally started in the carpet industry before David became a scrap metal dealer. They invested their money in metals, such as aluminium and copper, before launching Trans World Metals in the 1990's. Their many business activities involve real estate, including London commercial properties. Their net worth equates to $14.4 bn, but their ventures have contributed to increases in GDP, employment, and industry infrastructure.

PHILIP GREEN

Green was a high street retail mogul, whose rise originated from taking a £20,000 loan when he was 21 to sell jeans. He was known for having a ruthless bargaining style, and led the Arcadia Group, which owned brands like Topshop and British Home Stores (BHS) in the UK. Eventually due to lack of modernisation, and Green taking too many personal dividends out of his businesses, the companies collapsed and the pension fund was left with a huge black hole, which Green was forced to partially fill from his own accumulated wealth.

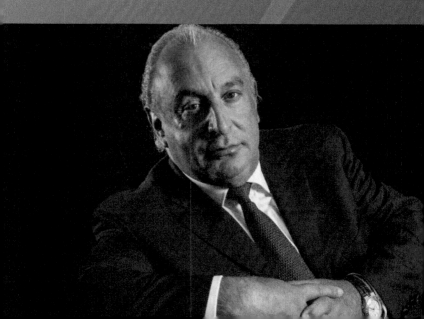

Opportunity recognition

For an opportunity to be entrepreneurial it must possess the ability to succeed into the future, an aspirational outcome that is possible through growth and change. The entrepreneur must also truly believe that an opportunity can meet this outcome (Stevenson & Gumpert, 1985).

In recognising an opportunity, an entrepreneur will scan the economic environment looking for changes that offer an opportunity. In terms of innovation, it may not be about creating something new, but adapting something old. Entrepreneurs will often turn perceived problems into opportunities for growth. For example, in terms of technology, advances in technology for the microcomputer shrank the mini-computer market. Whilst one market was depleting another market was rising. Shifts in production to the developing markets would mean the entrepreneur has taken hold of an opportunity. Another opportunity arose with consumer economics. For example, understanding what consumers can afford, or whether a rise in domestic energy prices may spark an opportunity to produce wood burning stoves. This argument is simplified given the pressures we are now seeing on energy prices and sustainability.

Other aspects to consider are changing consumer trends and government policies which could restrict emissions or the deregulation of the air industry, giving consumer's additional choice and entrepreneurs a chance to enter the industry (Stevenson and Gumpert, 1985).

In corporate settings, executives may avoid risky opportunities as they are less likely to be disciplined for missing an opportunity compared to the executive who follows an idea that fails.

Corporations may see change as failure of planning and process, whilst the entrepreneur is keen to embrace and exploit the opportunities these new directions hold. Resources for an entrepreneurial venture may be scarce. Rather than using high amounts of resources to make a venture succeed, an entrepreneur will often make their resources as efficient as possible to meet the needs of the opportunity (Stevenson and Gumpert,1985).

Dana (1995) takes a different approach in understating opportunity recognition by the entrepreneur. He posits the view that entrepreneurs consider opportunities based on their environmental setting. Entrepreneurship should not just be viewed as a function of opportunity, "but as a function of cultural perceptions of opportunity". On studying Eskimos in a remote arctic village, Dana (1995) categorises entrepreneurs into groups based on their individual experiences. The categories are not exhaustive and are highly applicable to the study undertaken by Dana (1995), however they provide an insight into cultural differentiations.

DANA'S (1995) CULTURAL VARIATIONS OF THE ENTREPRENEUR

Category of Entrepreneur	Key Defining Elements	Key Words	Type of Entrepreneurship
Traditional Self-Employed	Risk of economic uncertainty; no technology or innovation involved	Risk ; adventure; uncertainty	Opportunity seeking
Cultural Entrepreneur	Culturally acquired values such as thrift, asceticism and frugality	Work ethic; thrift; frugal; culture	Opportunity seeking
Personality Determined Achiever	Specific psychological traits such as high need for achievement	Independence; be my own boss; need to achieve	Opportunity seeking
Barthian Agent	Visible social impact on community	Social change; transformed the community	Opportunity seeking
Hagenian Displacee	Social displacement resulting in self-employment	Lost my job; got fired; unemployed; bored; welfare	Reactive (to displacement)
Kirznerian Identifier	Identification of an existing market opportunity	Opportunity; stumbled across; accident	Reactive (to displacement)

Four out of the six categories are opportunity-seeking type entrepreneurs (see above), whilst two groups are entrepreneurs due to a change in environment that forces them to behave differently. Some cultures have a higher representation of entrepreneurs than others, whilst in some society's entrepreneurship is not desirable, although these communities will welcome externals to carry out entrepreneurial tasks (Becker, 1956).

Personality-determined achiever

The personality-determined achiever is defined by McCelland's (1961) work on n achievement personalities. The view that some personalities are driven by the need to achieve will encourage them to demonstrate entrepreneurial traits.

The small business owner may not necessarily be classed as an entrepreneur, as a conventional definition of the entrepreneur is someone utilising a venture for profit and growth. Whilst the small business owner is interested in achieving personal goals and will often be involved in a single venture that occupies much of their time (Carland, Hoy, Boulton and Carland, 1984). In understanding the difference between the entrepreneur and the small business owner, growth alone is not a conclusive measure. However, entrepreneurs may move towards seeking growth (Begley, 1995).

Moreover, an entrepreneur specifically known as a Barthian agent is not necessarily categorised by the actions of owning a small business. The Barthian agent concerns the impact made in a society or culture. The entrepreneur can communicate with two societies whereby one is economically more advanced than the other. The entrepreneur can introduce entrepreneurial technological ideas or thoughts into the environment that is less advanced. The Barthian agent is less applicable to societies that are highly developed. The Barthian agent may be better placed in a society that follows the same set of values, such as an ethnic group. The group may also be biologically self-sustainable, communicative, interactive and distinguishable against any other group through their identity (Barth, 1969).

The Hagenian Displacee is the view that marginal outsiders when entering a society are not considered relatively important or high in terms of their status in the adopted society. Entrepreneurship can be used as a compensation toll for low social status (Hagen, 1962).

The Kirznerian Identifier concerns the economical equilibrium of society. The view that entrepreneur's new innovations will cause disequilibrium in the short term as they look for new profit opportunities and society takes time to adjust. The difference in existing views of the causes of disequilibrium is that the Kirznerian identifier is not causing new disequilibrium, but more reacting to opportunities for existing disequilibrium (Kirzner, 1973).

Dana (1995) finds that in Arctic towns, Eskimos are less likely to become entrepreneurs than non-native type people. With only 7.1% of a sample of native people saying they would look for profit seeking initiatives.

This indicates that there are unique cultural causes as to why the natives may not be entrepreneurial. In the wider environment, this would suggest that defining entrepreneurship based on opportunity may be too confined in some cases. The perception of culture should be taken into consideration when looking at entrepreneurial opportunities. In terms of the Eskimo environment, increasing the supply of entrepreneurs in the setting will not be a solution due to the culture of not seeking profit. Teaching and offering guidance on the spirit of entrepreneurship may elicit future entrepreneurial talent, while government legislation could spark reactive entrepreneurship in order to solve a problem (Dana, 1995).

Entrepreneurial opportunities are not transparent. They are entrepreneurial because they are not always clear at the time of discovery. These opportunities whether new or an adaptation of an existing product or service are unique because of their future uncertainty. They cannot be easily predicted as they demonstrate a level of future uncertainty (Baumol, 1993). Entrepreneurial opportunities may be uncovered when resources are deemed to be underutilised. Prices for goods may be too low and, if sold in another form or market, may yield a higher price. Not taking advantage of this will in effect cause an entrepreneurial loss as an opportunity has not been exploited. Consequently, acting on this opportunity in the wrong way will also generate a loss (Casson, 1982).

To a large extent entrepreneurship may rely on information asymmetry. When one or two entrepreneurs are aware of an innovation, there exists an opportunity for profit and growth potential. However, when a number of entrepreneurs receive information on the innovation, more and more competition can enter the market. This starts to make the original opportunity less profitable and less exclusive, therefore the desire to pursue is reduced (Baltar & Couldon, 2014).

Whilst there may be opportunities to exploit, a decision to take the opportunity must be decided. Also, the nature and impact of the opportunity may increase the willingness to engage in the opportunity. For example, the impact on society, the status generated, or the profit potential (Kirzner, 1973). Furthermore, individual differences in the entrepreneur may make them avoid or take on certain opportunities. In recognising the value generated through the opportunity, this may be compared against the cost required to support the opportunity. Other individual differences may be in assessing the venture's risk of failure versus its chance of success (Shane & Venkataraman, 2000).

Successful entrepreneurs will often recognise a winning opportunity whilst failing entrepreneurs will often run out of funds before they have fully understood or cashed-in on their idea. Moreover, turning an idea into an opportunity needs to be thought through for the undertaking to be a success. A good idea may not be a good venture unless it has potential. Understanding what makes a good business proposition is described by the five anchors:

1. It adds value to the end user
2. It solves a real-life problem that existing solutions may not yet have achieved
3. There is a need or a sense of urgency The product, for example, provides a solution quickly and is effective enough for customers to make quick decisions
4. The entrepreneur can prove the

product/service has realistic and potentially versatile profit-making ability across or in a set market
5. The entrepreneur has the given skill-set or experience to support the opportunity

The five anchors are about exploiting a window of opportunity, whereby there is a perfect period to launch, establish, and profit from a product or service. An opportunity needs to add value, fix a problem and, ultimately, be tempting for customers to spark an impulse or essential mind-set purchase. A successful entrepreneur may review first what the customer wants, what exists in the market already, and build an offering that creates competitive advantage based on improving factors that exist already (Spinelli & Adams, 2010).

ELON MUSK

ON OPPORTUNITY
RECOGNITION
& ACHIEVEMENT

One of the most prolific entrepreneurs of modern times is Elon Musk. From the above table, we might assume that he is the personality-determined achiever. However, in recognising his choices in his entrepreneurial exploits, he looked at industries in which many believed he would not be successful. But, this is where there are unique opportunities to exploit (Musk, 2014). In Elon's mind it's more than likely he possesses drivers that cause him to be a Barthian Agent, seeking to improve or develop humanity.

Some of these projects are big and highly impactful. He believes you should also identify projects where you will have high success combined with making a positive impact. It's no secret that many of Musk's projects are controversial, backed by huge investment and face tough challenges to advance. But, this tenacity to see the long-term vision is what makes some of Musk's visionary ideas have longevity.

Many may not understand his views or goals, but for Elon there is likely to be razor sharp focus in the way he conducts his business practices. As Musk starts to play with Artificial Intelligence and enhance genomics, he remains aware of the impact of such advancement. Albeit that he remains unsure whether this will do more harm than good to humanity overall.

Creativity

Zaleznick and Kets de Vries (1976) research is underpinned by the view that, even if not exhaustively, many entrepreneurial figures are entrepreneurial because of a lack of a father figure in their younger life. Their ability to be innovative and creative is linked to a desire to fill the gap where a father figure was missing or went away. The entrepreneur becomes engrossed in entrepreneurial ventures. Because of early childhood experiences the entrepreneur takes a leadership role because he or she finds it hard to relate to authority because of the vulnerable position they were placed in as a child. Moreover, if a child is abandoned by their father, they seek entrepreneurship as a way of building self-esteem. However, building a successful entrepreneurial firm may also play doubt in their mind because they may question the right to success because of their parental rejection. Modern development of this absence of a father figure may be purely contextual to the time. As social norms have developed, the same may be true for lack of a mother or nurturing figure within a family unit.

To conclude the topic of creativity, there may come a time when successful entrepreneurs outgrow a venture. Eventually some growing ventures will require a need for general management as opposed to an entrepreneurial visionary. Because of an entrepreneur's leadership style when a business grows to a certain point, chaos can erupt. An entrepreneur will take the stance of doing everything themselves rather than delegating. Becoming involved in mundane tasks will not allow them to have a strategic overview (Zaleznik & Kets de Vries, 1976).

ROB KALIN
AND ETSY

Rob Kalin, the founder of Etsy, follows one of the guiding principles of Steve Jobs. Namely, to look at oneself as an outsider, leaning into an organisation, or as an underdog. You should adopt this approach even more so as you become more successful. Kalin refers to himself as the 'Crafter in Chief'. Ideas such as maximising shareholder value are crazy ideals. As, after all, shareholder wealth would be maximised if things were done well anyway! In his quest to build Etsy, he adopts an anti-business rhetoric, trying to evolve and develop creativity (Dooley, 2023)

Etsy

Anxiety

Lynn (1969) on comparing entrepreneurs against general managers, finds that entrepreneurs tend to have more stressful lives than managers, as he or she is solely responsible for the whole project or venture and is battling competitive forces. As a result, in this sample, entrepreneurs elicited higher levels of neuroticism than general managers. Lynn (1969) concludes that there may be a link between creativity and neuroticism. Baron's (1963), work on creative writers supports this view. As entrepreneurs are creative in nature, they too may share this link with creative writers. They are on a journey of innovation and growth and may become anxious in putting ideas and opportunities into practice. Anxiety or neuroticism may form part of the entrepreneur's personality (Lynn, 1969).

The undertakings of an entrepreneur are inherently risky and hold an uncertain future, as discussed in the literature. Because of this, the entrepreneur's life remains delicate. One success could be followed by a failure. Some entrepreneurs may go from being highly successful and wealthy to losing it all due to ill planning of the next future and poor long-term investment. As discussed in Zaleznik and

Kets de Vries's (1976) work, much of these failures are because of poor family relationships in the past. Those entrepreneurs with a turbulent family past will look for structure and focus highly on a particular venture or enterprise.

However, due to their experiences of losing a father for example, they are aware that this rejection and heartache can mean, in an entrepreneurial sense, they are not worthy of success and failure is bound to happen. However, this reactive behaviour can also play homage to the entrepreneur's personality in the resilient way in which they deal with problems and drawbacks in their venture.

Following on from McClelland's (1961) work on reaching a definition of the entrepreneur under n achievement, using the same testing apparatus, Collins and Moore (1964,) find that the entrepreneur:

1. Suffers from a lack of rational reasoning, concerned with being successful or more successful
2. Leads subordinates
3. Avoids or dislikes authority

4. Is anxious and self-destructive

In understanding the entrepreneur and his anxious behaviour, his childhood can unlock an understanding of why he is how he is. An entrepreneur's ambition for success may be a reaction against anxiety. If an entrepreneur was rejected by a fatherly figure, either by them leaving or not being present whilst growing up, ambition may counteract feelings of helplessness in a previous situation. The entrepreneur reacts to early feelings experienced in his family settings or childhood (Zaleznik & Kets de Vries, 1976).

In being successful, the entrepreneur will not feel accomplished. He is always faced with the stresses of his past. He or she will often bring these past experiences to the foreground of their entrepreneurial life. This can create anxiety as, whatever they experienced, whether this is rejection or a bad relationship with an authority figure, they will always feel hostile towards those who hold positions of authority. When there is indeed success this may be counteracted with the anxiety of future failures and vice versa due to experiences of rejection and feelings of insecurity (Kets de Vries, 1977).

Kets de Vries (1985) extends this understanding to entrepreneurship in general. As the entrepreneur pushes for an optimistic outlook if his venture fails, he will see this as payment for much of the time being successful. In effect, relieving anxiety, knowing all ventures can lead to some sort of positive outlook.

Being unburdened by the pressures of the failing venture, the entrepreneur can move on to the next venture with energy and drive (Kets de Vries, 1985).

Many entrepreneurs work under caution that too much success leads to failure and, as a result, can make them anxious. (Kets de Vries, 1985). In terms of anxiety management, some entrepreneurs react to anxiety by taking action, often less rational than normal, because of their anxious mind-set (Kets de Vries, 1985).

KARREN BRADY

ON MAINTAINING CONTROL

Notorious Entrepreneur Karren Brady, quotes; 'Women have brains and uteruses, and are able to use both". After discovering very suddenly she had a brain aneurysm, she didn't panic. She broke it down into 5 stages. 1: finding out what she had; 2: understanding the different treatment options; 3: choosing the treatment; 4: having the treatment; and, 5: finally moving on with her life. Within a day, she was responding to emails. Now this style is not for everyone and may seem like a very business-like approach to continuing life after a very shocking diagnosis. However, the process for which to break down tasks, events or problems, allows us to add a controlled perspective and remove anxiety about situations (Cochrane, 2010).

Control

For individuals who demonstrate entrepreneurial characteristics, whether in a corporation or working for themselves, it has been found that a sense of individual success is maintained through maintaining a sense of freedom and responsibility. However, this is not to say an entrepreneur cannot feel successful when they work in a group, if they contribute to a successful outcome and are able to track their support and understand how well they have done (McClelland, 1961).

A major function of the entrepreneur is their ability to coordinate within their venture. There has been some debate on whether this is classed as a management function, and there has been no evidence to suggest successful entrepreneurs have high coordination skills, although they have been shown to contribute to organisational efficiency (McClelland, 1961).

AMERICAN EXPRESS

1 Combine physical spaces

If you're the entrepreneur, then centre the company around you. Shared office spaces provide a no brainer economy of scale, this also provides an opportunity to share resources on projects. Better still, if you can have remote working capabilities, your workforce can work anywhere in the world, even in shared environments. Through principles such as Agile, you can get your teams dispatched to work on multiple different projects at any one time.

2 Bring business processes together

Many ideas are generated in isolation and can't be combined with other principles. However, having shared functions like marketing, finance or operational processes, means that you can streamline areas of expertise, rather than wasting time, effort and money on duplicating functions across different brands or functions.

AMERICAN EXPRESS

3 Prioritise what needs your attention over anything else

Your time is probably the most important and it's likely you are spreading yourself very thin across multiple meetings and engagements. Consider what the most important tasks are that you must achieve before anything else. It may not always be the best tasks or the most enjoyable ones that you conquer but consider not always doing the things you enjoy...decide what is most practical.

4 Don't overthink the small stuff

If your focus and vision are maintained, don't overthink the small problems that arise during entrepreneurial undertakings. If you turn these into bigger problems, then they may derail your efforts. Treat them as part of the journey and continue to fix forward. If the issue doesn't affect the ongoing equilibrium of your journey, then it's fine to continue.

5 Make lists and follow them

There are many ways to create lists. These can be written down or digitised for use wherever you are across a range of devices. Whilst managing many aspects of multiple businesses, it's important to keep track of your ventures and understand tasks that need to be completed.*

*However, I recently spoke to an entrepreneurial fashion designer, who opts for a more organic approach to understanding what needs to be done. It's true that if you clear your mind of distractions, then things that need to be completed come naturally without the need for a to-do list, and this also increases creative opportunities.

6 Use time tracking tools for your multiple businesses

This one is not necessarily about tracking productivity and the effectiveness of the workforce. It helps to determine if you're balancing time effectively across multiple ventures and, as a by-product, can show you where there are productivity issues. But this should not be the main goal! For a meatier approach to this analysis, you can grab some great productivity tools that analyse where improvements can be made.

7 Keep reports on each business, understand accountability

Report maintenance is key, analysing accounts and contracts allow you to stay legal, build growth plans and ultimately work out the integrity, legitimacy and future longevity of your empire.

8 Work with your co-founding teams to understand balance and accountability

Work with your co-founding team to establish who does what and, if you have multiple businesses, how much time and effort you can really give to that venture. Everyone's expectations of one another are bound to be different, so it's important to align on a continuous basis. Especially before you bring in external parties. It's important to remember that no one is you, people will work hard for you, but they may not have the same vision or drivers as yours. Before you employ, be very clear on why they are there and what their purpose is.

9 Bring experts in for things you don't know

This one seems and appears to be self-explanatory, however it's not. Many entrepreneurial individuals will believe that they can do everything themselves. Unfortunately, this is not the case. You will have a unique set of skills that you should focus on but, if you really don't know something, it's worth your time and effort to engage a professional in a particular field, such as accounting. It's sometimes advisable to seek guidance from someone who has key knowledge too, acting on recommendations are often the elements that keep your business together, and can be the difference between success and failure.*

*On a regular basis, I meet with the co-founders of one of my companies. We often ask what our accountabilities are and it's surprising how much this changes throughout the year (American Express, 2017).

Rebellion

Underdeveloped economies to some degree are said to rely on the entrepreneur. Traditional values in these societies may allow entrepreneurs to flourish, but other values may not. Industrial entrepreneurs arise in societies where industrial activity is valued as having low importance and are regarded as rebels in society. Hagen's (1961) research explores the traditional views of society in Latin America. He finds that whilst there is money to be made in many entrepreneurial ventures, traditional views concern the ideology of making a dignified living. Whilst a saloon may generate more money than any other business in a town, the traditional view is no individual wants to make money from such business undertakings due to its low working status. The entrepreneur, therefore, becomes a rebel to society by not conforming. Of course, Public Houses and Saloons are considered a reputable way to make money now, and the norms of entrepreneurial undertakings have developed greatly over the past 60 years!

VIVIENNE WESTWOOD

Vivienne Westwood, an acclaimed designer, rewrote the fashion rulebook and, on many occasions, stayed true to anti-establishment values. She remained true to her values throughout her life. She maintained the position of rebellion using fashion as a form of self-expression. She hated a world of torture and death, as prompted by the problems in the western world, and protested in a way through her clothes. The clothes moved with the times but maintained the same rhetoric (Beresford, 2023).

Entrepreneurial schools of thought

Operating or owning some form of business or venture is often the driver for being classified as an entrepreneur, as indeed is taking on a project. However, Cunningham & Lischeron (1991) argue that, whilst entrepreneurial definitions unite, there are several viewpoints when it comes to understanding what an entrepreneur is. They take six schools of thought when breaking down the unified definition. Within these six schools of thought many of the characteristics of a perceived entrepreneur are unpacked and can be broken down further into four categories:

Assessing Personal Qualities
1. The "Great Person" School of Entrepreneurship
2. The Psychological Characteristics School of Entrepreneurship

Recognising Opportunities
 3. The Classical School of Entrepreneurship

<u>Acting and Managing</u>
4. The Management School of
Entrepreneurship
5. The Leadership School of Entrepreneurship

<u>Reassessing and Adapting</u>
 6.The Intrapreneurship School of
Entrepreneurship

The perceived characteristics of the
entrepreneur at certain points of the lifecycle
of a venture are likely to differentiate.
Cunningham & Lischeron (1991) summarise
the relevant characteristics demonstrated in
the table below (Cunningham & Lischeron,
1991, p.46).

SUMMARY OF APPROACHES FOR DESCRIBING ENTREPRENEURSHIP

Entrepreneurial Model	Central Focus on Purpose	Assumption	Behaviours and Skills	Situation
"Great Person School"	The entrepreneur has an intuitive ability--a sixth sense and traits and instincts he/she is born with	Without this "inborn" intuition the individual would be like the rest of us mortals who 'lack what it takes'	Intitution, vigour, energy, persistence & self-esteem	Start-up
Psychological Characterstics School	Entrepreneurs have unique values, attitudes & needs which drive them	People behave in accordance with their values, behaviour results from attempts to satisfy needs	Personal values risk taking, need for achievement & others	Start-up
Classical School	The central characteristic of entrepreneurial behaviour is innovation	The critical aspect of entrepreneurship is in the process of doing rather than owning	Intention, creativity & discovery	Start-up & early growth
Management School	Entrepreneurs are organisers of an economic venture, they are people who organise, own manage & assume the risk	Entrepreneurs can be developed and trained in the technical functions of management	Product planning, capitalisation and budgeting	Early growth & maturity
Leadership School	Entrepreneurs are leaders of people; they have the ability to adapt their style to the needs of people	An entrepreneur cannot accomplish his/her goals alone but depends on others	Motivating, directing & leading	Early growth & maturity
Interpreneurship School	Entrepreneurial skills can be useful in complex organisations. Interpreneurship is the development of independent units to create market, and expand services	Organisations need to adapt to survive. Entrepreneurial activity leads to organisational building and entrepreneurs becoming managers	Alertness to opportunities maximising decisions	Maturity & change

"The Great Person" School of Entrepreneurship

This is based on the understanding of whether entrepreneurs are born with entrepreneurial talent or whether they learn their skills and develop their acumen. This view is that some individuals are 'great people' in that they demonstrate a natural born talent. These types of characteristics are likely to be elicited at the start of the venture and are particularly applicable to this research in determining the success of a venture.

This entrepreneur may act upon their inner thoughts and emotions, believing that they possess the right course of action. The individual will also possess the drive for success. The typical ideology of a "Great Person" school is that they are likely to have the most desirable appearances, those that society views as physically attractive, contributing to making this kind of entrepreneur aspirational to others in who they are and what they do.

The Psychological Characteristics School of Entrepreneurship

This school of entrepreneurship presents the view that individuals have deep psychological attitudes towards how they act in work and life. The view that entrepreneurial people will have a desire to act in an entrepreneurial way doing entrepreneurial tasks over those who do not. Three personality characteristics have been given the most attention in this school of thought: the personal values of the individual, including integrity, ethical stance and responsibility. The second thought is the natural intrinsic value to take risks that lend themselves to someone's personality. And finally, the need and potential want for achievement (Cunnigham & Lischeron, 1991).

In terms of personal values of the entrepreneur, there are many desirable personality traits that would be socially acceptable. However, more entrepreneurs than not demonstrate high ethical practice and are deemed to be socially responsible in comparison to the general population. This school of thought does not believe that entrepreneurship can be taught in a classroom setting. Rather, it is a development of personality over time stemming from early childhood relationships with educational teachers and parents. The ideas and values created in a child's early years are what remain in mind making decisions and causing actions throughout life. General values will remain the same and guide the individual's decision-making in all situations (Belshaw, 1955). The need for achievement can be traced back to early childhood. Those expected to achieve outside of the home in earlier years did so with a higher impact than children who were encouraged in much later years. However, encouraging and pushing children to achieve may actually be damaging to their achievement orientation as they may lack the mental capability. Whilst encouragement too late may mean they have passed the period when values can be enforced. The suggested ages for optimisation of achievement reinforcement is between ages six and eight (Winterbottom, 1958).

When understanding risk taking attitudes, Mill (1984), in terms of entrepreneurship, argues that risk taking levels are what differentiates a manager and an entrepreneur, relating to financial, career options and family life (Liles 1974; Sarachek, 1978). Despite the understanding that there is an element of risk taking involved, it is not to be cast aside that the risk is potentially systematic, in that it is likely to lead to profit generation (McClelland & Winter, 1969). In line with the different schools of thought, the classical school of thought argues that once the innovative process or project development stage has ceased and the venture has become established, then perhaps the entrepreneurial traits have been minimised (Kilby, 1971).

The last personality trait associated with this school is the need for achievement. Whilst many may seek the need for achievement in academic, professional or personal contexts, largely due to their environment. A protestant's value is that an individual is judged on their accomplishment, and therefore there may be a strong desire to achieve (McClelland, Atkinson, Clark & Lowell, 1976). It would be wrong to isolate the need to start a business on the merit of the need to achieve. The desire to move away from the confinements of working in a corporate environment is also considered under this school (Hull, Bosle & Udell, 1980).

This school of thought is deemed to be present in the early stages of entrepreneurial start-ups (Cunnigham & Lischeron, 1991). This school raises the idea that there are certain personality traits that are needed to be an entrepreneur, and that these are demonstrated very early in life, causing a smaller window of cultivation, where there is a strong need for achievement, risk taking and eliciting type A behaviour. (Beagley and Boyd, 1987).

The Classical School of Entrepreneurship

The classical school of entrepreneurship raises the viewpoint of understanding and decoding what is meant by the term entrepreneurship, raising the ideology that the core meaning of the word provides a differentiation between managers and entrepreneurs. The route meaning of entrepreneurs originates from the French word "entreprendre" meaning to undertake. In the sixteenth century entrepreneurs were regarded as those who undertook activity much like military expeditions. Extending the military context, in the 1700's the term also included those who were involved in military building and the construction of roads, bridges, and harbours. French economists also used the term in describing individuals that bear risk and increase uncertainty for the success of innovative projects (de Farcy, 1973). These definitions together encompass a form of entrepreneurial undertaking in which there are both risk and innovative elements involved (Cunnigham & Lischeron, 1991). Furthermore, those individuals who are seen to look for certain outcomes are unlikely to be successful entrepreneurs according to Drucker (2007).

More recently there has been much confusion in describing the term of entrepreneurship under this school. In 1885, the Oxford English Dictionary described the term as "the director or manager of a public institution... a contractor acting as an intermediary between capital and labour". Both definitions raise the understanding of talented entrepreneurial-like individuals but exclude the element of risk. Moreover, these definitions play favour to the view that entrepreneurship is more about the process of "doing" rather than the "owning" of the business (Herbert & Link, 1982). In addition Schumpeter (1934) believes that entrepreneurship lies in the innovative approach to the task or project, disregarding the need for ownership (Schumpeter, 1934).

The Classical school of entrepreneurship is underpinned by innovation, creativity and discovery. In this school, entrepreneurship concerns creating or discovering an opportunity to elicit entrepreneurial skills. Whilst this view on entrepreneurship is deemed simplistic, it is often met with resistance, especially when creative tasks may be categorised as non-conformance or a desire to exert personality. Some discoveries may, at first, elicit resistance. For example, theories from Darwin, Galieilo, and Newton were not welcomed during the early stages (Cunnigham & Lischeron, 1991).

Moreover, the innovative nature of the entrepreneur through their creative activity may fulfil personal desires and avoid the need of the wider social environment. Some entrepreneurs may not be interested in public opinion or reaction to their innovative advancements (Cunnigham & Lischeron, 1991).

This kind of behaviour, despite its grandeur and opportunity to create entrepreneurial success, may also lead to disaster.

The Management School of Entrepreneurship

Management theory provides much evidence for entrepreneurship. Original management school definitions are based on logic and as a result have been widely accepted. Original assumptions are based on the ideology that managers perform a variety of tasks under management operations including planning, budgetary control, and human resources. Under this school an entrepreneur is an individual who organises or manages a business-undertaking, assuming the risk for the sake of profit (Webster 1966). There is also a level of supervision, control and direction (Mill, 1984; Lischeron, 1991). Supplementary to this, there is specific text that outlines the start-up, strategy and development growth that entrepreneurs become involved in (Good 1989). Other writers in the school of management outline the movement from being an entrepreneur to being a professional manager. Whereby the manner of responsibility and delegation takes place as well as the sense of control across these delegations (Roberts, 1987). University students who can be defined as new or potential entrepreneurs of the future, study using textbooks that are designed primarily for a corporate environment, where the principal subject matter may be similar (Vesper, 1985).

The management school approach is based on technicality and supports the view that entrepreneurs can be trained and coached in the classroom. Start-up ventures fail possibly due to knowledge and suitable decision making. Further to this, lacking knowledge in management, finance and marketing may contribute to failure. This school promotes the view that entrepreneurship is a set of skills that can contribute to the management of a venture. Because the management school is based on improving an individual's management capability, and on the basis that entrepreneurs can be taught, the specific aim is to provide support in entrepreneurial functions. Courses that provide essential new venture marketing and finance are beneficial (Boberg,1988). Skill enhancement should lead to reductions in venture failure.

The Leadership School of Entrepreneurship

In understanding entrepreneurship, an entrepreneur is often a leader with the power to lead others. The leadership school takes a non-technical stance in understanding entrepreneurs. This school supports the view that the entrepreneur must be a leader in their approach, being able to lead others, and motivate them into understanding the cause. As well as this they must be able to communicate a clear approach to what they want to achieve whilst acting as a role model to others with the ability to coach and mentor the experience they have (Kao 1989).

The leadership school takes two viewpoints when dealing with the entrepreneurial leader. The first viewpoint is based on the "great person" leader, and emphasises that personality traits, such as willingness, cooperativeness and recognition of responsibility, will enable entrepreneurs to be adaptive in a variety of situations contributing to driving success (Stogdill, 1974 & Bass, 1981).

The second viewpoint is based on understanding how an entrepreneurial leader "makes things happen" responding to the needs and wants of people in their environment. Completing tasks are of joint concern for an enterprise – for those doing the work and the task that needs to be completed (Hemphill, 1959). It is suggested that both these concerns are important and for the leader they should attempt to adjust their leadership style, depending on the relationship with which they are faced (Fiedler, 1966). Entrepreneurial leadership, besides other personality traits, may involve outlining clear targets and goals and setting venture direction through people-empowerment and human resource implementation (Kao, 1989).

Entrepreneurs according to this school are "social architects", capable of promoting strong values, principles, and beliefs (Bennis and Nanus, 1985).

Research from this school calls upon those who lead and those who exert management control. Entrepreneurs are capable of leading or destroying venture development by their entrepreneurial desires of leading success and being an entrepreneur. However, regardless of the complex nature of the entrepreneur, the most effective leaders are those that can set clear visions for their employees or company, develop commitment, and promote engagement (Bennis and Nanus, 1985).

The leadership belief is that entrepreneurs will be good mentors and effective in developing others around them (Levinson et al. 1978). The leader may have gained experience and be a professional in their entrepreneurial talent, passing this to others through knowledge transfer. The entrepreneurial mentoring process is so important that the manager will act in a leadership capacity (Carsrund et al. 1986).

The Intrapreneurship School of Entrepreneurship

The Intrapreneurship school of entrepreneurship has been developed to conquer the low level of innovativeness found in organisations. Individuals are given freedom of ideas within a corporate structure and can use entrepreneurial talents to expand ideas, allowing the corporation's activity to be extended without the individual's need or risk of ownership (Ellis and Taylor, 1987). As well as this, potential diversification within a company is accessible (Burgelman, 1983).

Intrapreneurship is created by developing inner business groups that are responsible for innovation, expanding, and developing new technological methods within an organisation (Nielsen et al. 1985).

There is some debate as to why this school should be included within entrepreneurial definitions, as entrepreneurship has often fallen in parallel with organisational structures. However, Schumpeter (1934) believes that the development of entrepreneurs often leads to management capability.

The school raises the idea that entrepreneurial innovation can be expressed within existing organisations by working in innovative units. Despite these units, they have often proved unsuccessful with entrepreneurs seeking to leave to start their own ventures due to frustration (Knight, 1988), suggesting incompatibility with normal corporate management styles and structure.

Intrapreneurship seems to flourish when entrepreneurial skills are used to the advantage of both the individual and the company, and there is an allowance for opportunities to exert entrepreneurial behaviours.

The model itself allows for greater freedom within a workplace setting to develop entrepreneurial innovativeness. Because of the business unit, entrepreneurs may be required to work in teams more often than they would desire. There is a strong element of teamwork involved, understanding, and engaging with other people's ideas. Building the correct team, to utilise everyone's skills is important (Echert et al., 1991).

Fundamentally whilst Intrapreneurship can create freedom of ideas it can also drive "bureaucratic creativity".

Intrapreneurship units can work on strategic development, product development and operational efficiency. The team may require the use of professionals and operational support throughout projects. The goal of each unit will require responsibility, team working and the ability to elicit ownership and drive

success using entrepreneurial traits
(Cunnigham & Lischeron, 1991).

Selecting and understanding the appropriate school of thought

The above entrepreneurial schools of thought handle defining entrepreneurship from a variety of different angles. The first viewpoint attempts to define entrepreneurship through personality traits and beliefs, whilst the second angle realises that seeking opportunities and understanding the future is crucial to entrepreneurship. The third angle suggests that entrepreneurial skill can be enhanced by technical and non-technical skill enhancement. This also raises the support of experienced entrepreneurs acting as mentors for new entrepreneurs or those with less experience.

The research above does not attempt to rule a particular school of thought superior over another (see below). The definitions outlined below recognise the schools of thought discussed, however are not exhaustive to the varying definitions of entrepreneurship. The classical school pushes for venture creation through seeking opportunities and gauging creativity, whilst the psychological school raises the importance of certain entrepreneurial behaviours such as risk-taking propensity as well as the need for achievement. The management school raises the view of increasing technical business acumen of entrepreneurs, strengthening their knowledge to initiate business success. The leadership school concerns those leadership characteristics that will motivate and drive people to achieve. Whilst intrapreneurship is keen to promote entrepreneurial innovativeness from inside corporate settings.

Each school of thought addresses a wide range of perspectives, understanding personal values and beliefs through to deciding appropriate entrepreneurial actions to drive ventures forward. The table below suggests that the process of entrepreneurial development is repetitive and carried out in a step-by-step manner. The psychological schools and "Great person" school of thought gains strength by acting as an assessor, providing a personal assessment of an entrepreneur and understanding the personality traits for success. These schools of thought should not outline the perfect entrepreneur as this would be subjective. They may act as a tool of self-comparison between an individual and a deemed successful entrepreneur in understanding what has contributed to their success in terms of personality, principles, and beliefs. Other schools understand the importance of ideas, and act upon these ideas. Management and leadership schools introduce the sets of skills that may be desirable and beneficial to elicit entrepreneurship and the tools needed to motivate others.

Intrapreneurship is important as it recognises that at some point in a venture's life cycle, there is need for change in strategic direction to continue. Whilst the assumption is that schools operate independently, as the table below shows, there is a continuous process of potential re-evaluation of where an entrepreneur sits. Whilst an entrepreneur may not pass chronologically through all definitions, they can draw upon some if not all the basic assumptions.

Selecting the best entrepreneurial definition to follow may be decided based on the appropriateness of the task and the research and assumptions that need to be tested. The management school of thought may be chosen to support the ideas of mentoring entrepreneurs.

However, to assume that an entrepreneur is created through the ideology of just one school would be far too simplistic. Ensuring the separate angles of entrepreneurship are covered may be more beneficial in defining the entrepreneur (Cunnigham & Lischeron, 1991).

SUMMARY OF CRITERIA OF EACH ENTREPRENEURIAL SCHOOL

Entrepreneurial Model	Definition	Measures	Questions
"Great Person"	"Extraordinary Achievers"	Personal Principles Personal histories Experiences	What principles do you have? What are your achievements?
Psycological Characterstics School	Founder control over the means of production	Locus of control Tolerance of ambiguity Need for achievement	What are your values?
Classical	People who make innovation bearing risk and uncertainty 'Creative destruction'	Decision making Abilities to see opportunities Creativity	What are the opportunities? What was your vision? How did you respond?
Management	Creating value through the recognition of business opportunity, the management of risk taking through the communicative and management skill to mobilise...	Expertise Technical knowledge Technical plans	What are your plans? What are your capabilities? What are your credentials?
Leadership	"Social architect" Promotion and protection of values	Attitudes, style Management of people	How do you manage people?
Interpreneurship	Those who pull together to promote innovation	Decision making	How do you change and adapt?

The side hustle

The side hustle needs to play an important part of the equation here because it's so prominent in modern society. A side hustle can be classified as another business undertaking that supports a regular source of income, such as having a full-time employment role. The side hustle is designed to support the ongoing costs of living and to increase opportunities to make extra cash. Everyone is trying to escape the rat race. However, having a side hustle keeps you in the rat race because you are effectively working more.

The side hustle provides an opportunity for you to become an entrepreneur. This is because the side hustle is an opportunity to do something different with your spare time. If you find that it is an effective way of earning income, you can transition from your main job to the side hustle. Therefore, what a side hustle is doing to your mind, is allowing you to think outside the box and try new things. It's very important to allow your mind to understand that there are other opportunities out there for you to expand into and realise that you don't need to focus on doing what everyone else does, thereby challenging the status quo.

How do entrepreneurs learn?

Learning remains crucially important in any task we undertake. It is the process of learning that creates knowledge. There must be a process in place to physically learn something. Broadly, an entrepreneur can learn how to do something through two mediums. This isn't isolated to entrepreneurs but applies to everyone (Gupta et. Al., 2006). The first medium is explorative learning, the second is exploitative. If an entrepreneur lacks the required skills, they are said to seek the resources necessary to gain the required knowledge to complete the task or project (Belshaw, 1955).

Entrepreneurs are said to favour an explorative style of learning, where they seek to understand or develop a concept themselves. This allows them to develop a concept at greater length but will often put greater stress on them initially. An exploitative style of learning is learning from a teacher or reading from a textbook. The only negative element of exploitative learning is that the knowledge is fixed to a point. Sometimes there is a need for both learning styles, especially when you do not have the time to learn something it is better to exploit the knowledge others provide to short-cut to the end goal. This is not often the case for the entrepreneur (Cope & Watts, 2000). Generally, entrepreneurs will learn to survive because their business undertakings depend on it.

However, because of this inherent independent nature, it could be a case of understanding what knowledge they require in their own context, rather than tailor one for all forms of support (Dalley & Hamilton, 2000).

So how can you be an entrepreneur?

There really is no hard and fast answer to this. Overall, I believe there are two things that can make you entrepreneurial. Firstly, its mindset. Are you looking for opportunities that seek to make you profit or solve a problem? Whatever drives you, whether it's your background or desire to be different or challenge the status quo, do not avoid that feeling, embrace it and use it in a positive way.

The second element of being an entrepreneur is your attitude to risk. Everything we do in life has an element of risk attached to it. But with risk generally comes reward. Quite simply, think about when you send that risky text asking a love interest something that's a little out there. They could either say no, or they could say yes. Risk is what underpins the financial system, it's there in the everyday decisions that we make. You will not succeed in life, in any way, shape, or form if you do not take risks. The level of risk you want to take is up to you and this measurement is different.

Personally, I live by the view of never wanting to look back and think, what-if. Others say risk what you can afford to lose.

We aren't just talking about money here. Your biggest resource is your time, choosing the right projects to undertake is not always easy. Often when it's ambiguous, if you believe you can win in an area, keep going. Remember to embrace your failures on the way to your success. Critics remark heavily on your failures and a lot less on your successes. This is not a self-help guide, more an understanding of what an entrepreneur is and how you may be able to get there yourself. However, here are the rules I follow in the form of business, social, and personal undertakings.

1. Not all aspects of your life can be good at the same time. When something is up, my working life can be stretched and vice versa. It's important to appreciate the positives when things are down

2. Not everyone will understand why you do the things you do. It doesn't matter – it's your path. Choose the opinions

you wish to listen to wisely, but also don't act like you know everything

3. In the same breath, many people will say "no" or "cannot". I've achieved a lot of "impossible" things, and there's still a long way to go!

4. Always listen to people that tell you that you can

5. You might not achieve your goals, but enjoying the journey is equally important

6. Sometimes you do have to take breaks. You can't be working on your goals all the time, so it's important to strike a balance

7. You know your limits. I can commit to a challenging and rewarding work career, but I find ways to escape. These escapes are truly unique for everyone

8. Be realistic, realise the level of commitment you have and accept that often you might need to compromise, but you genuinely can always find time

9. There will always be someone better, and there will always be someone who you think had it easier or does things in a way you can't understand. Don't get

jealous. Instead, use others to motivate yourself to improve and reach your goals

10. Be inspired. Mix your social circles, set role models for the person you want to be and use them to push you on

References

American Express. (2017). 9 Ways You Can Successfully Oversee Multiple Businesses. *Available at:* https://www.americanexpress.com/en-us/business/trends-and-insights/articles/9-ways-you-can-successfully-oversee-multiple-businesses/

Beresford, J. (2023). Vivienne Westwood: Rebel With A Cause.
Available at:
https://therake.com/stories/icons/vivienne-westwood-rebel-with-a-cause/

Branson, R. (2017). Richard Branson reveals the biggest business risks he's ever taken. *Available at:* https://www.independent.co.uk/news/business/indyventure/richard-branson-virgin-group-atlantic-records-biggest-business-risks-startup-entrepreneur-a7698711.html

CBS News (2017). For inventor Sir James Dyson, innovation is simple: "A lot of things don't work very well" *Available at:* https://www.cbsnews.com/news/sir-james-dyson-retail-store-cars-technology/

Cochrane, K. (2010). Karren Brady: 'Women have brains and uteruses and are able to use both".
Available at:
https://www.theguardian.com/football/2010/apr/11/karren-brady-west-ham-apprentice

Coleman, A. (2018). How Entrepreneurs Like Richard Branson Handle Business Risk. *Available at:* https://www.forbes.com/sites/alisoncoleman/2018/12/21/how-entrepreneurs-like-richard-branson-handle-business-risk/

Clifford, C (2017). What Richard Branson learned when Coke put Virgin Cola out of business. *Available at:* https://www.cnbc.com/2017/02/07/what-richard-branson-learned-when-coke-put-virgin-cola-out-of-business.html

Dikes, J (2022). What happened to the Dyson electric car? *Available at:* https://www.electrifying.com/blog/knowledge-hub/what-happened-to-the-dyson-electric-car#:~:text=So%2C%20what%20killed%20off%20the,going%20to%20be%20commercially%20viable

Dooley, R. (2023). Why Etsy's Rob Kalin Is Like Steve Jobs. *Available at:* https://www.neurosciencemarketing.com/blog/articles/etsy-rob-kalin-steve-jobs.htm

Landerman, B. (2019). Failing and Creating a Culture of Learning. *Available at:* https://aws.amazon.com/blogs/enterprise-strategy/failing-creating-a-culture-of-learning/

Mansor, D.J.D. (2017). Applying Rockefeller's Principles to Modern Day Business. *Available at:* https://www.linkedin.com/pulse/applying-rockefellers-principles-modern-day-business-david-mansor/

Moreton, C. (2010). 'I was selfish. I failed. And I've struggled with my conscience': The Apprentice's Lord Sugar looks back. *Available at:* https://www.dailymail.co.uk/home/moslive/article-1316206/The-Apprentices-Lord-Sugar-I-selfish-I-failed-And-Ive-struggled-conscience.html

Musk, E. (2014). Elon Musk on Seeking Opportunities. *Available at:* https://bigthink.com/words-of-wisdom/elon-musk-on-seeking-opportunities/

Philanthropy Roundtable. (2023). John Rockefeller Sr. *Available at:* https://www.philanthropyroundtable.org/hall-of-fame/john-rockefeller-sr/#:~:text=Within%20his%20lifetime%2C%20Rockefeller%20helped,China's%20first%20proper%20medical%20school.

Rhythmsystems, (2020). Richard Branson's Business Strategy: Proper Risk Taking. *Available at:* https://www.rhythmsystems.com/blog/take-risks-like-richard-branson#:~:text=Sir%20Richard%20believes%20that%20the,core%20business%20they%20started%20in.

United Arab Emirates Ministry of Economy. (2023). Entities supporting projects on Emirati Entrepreneurs. *Available at:* https://www.moec.gov.ae/en/entrepreneurship-support-entities#:~:text=Dozens%20of%20agencies%2C%20accelerators%20and,medium%20enterprises%20(SMEs)%20sector.

Vaswani, J. (2017). #10 Entrepreneurs Who are Bringing Change in the World. *Available at:* https://www.entrepreneur.com/en-in/entrepreneurs/10-entrepreneurs-who-are-bringing-change-in-the-world/292235

Notable works

Aboud, John and Hornaday, John A., Characteristics of Successful Entrepreneurs (1971). University of Illinois at Urbana-Champaign's Academy for Entrepreneurial Leadership Historical Research Reference in Entrepreneurship, *Available at :*
SSRN: https://ssrn.com/abstract=1505911

Aitken, H. G. J., The Future of Entrepreneurial Research (1963). University of Illinois at Urbana-Champaign's Academy for Entrepreneurial Leadership Historical Research Reference in Entrepreneurship, Available at SSRN: https://ssrn.com/abstract=1505224

Baty, G. 1981. Entrepreneurship for the Eighties

Begley, T.M. (1995). Using founder status, age of form, and company growth rate as the basis for distinguishing entrepreneurs from management of small businesses. *Journal of Business Venturing*, 10, (3), 249-263

Belshaw, C.S. (1955). The Cultural Milieu of the Entrepreneur: A Critical Essay. Exploration in Entrepreneurial History, 7(3), 146-163.

Bruyat, C. & Julient, P. (2000). Defining the fields of research in entrepreneurship. *Journal of Business Venturing*

Casson, M (1982). The Entrepreneur: An Economic Theory. Rowman & Littlefield

Cole, A.H. (1942) Entrepreneurship as an Area of Research. *Journal of Economic History Supplement*, 2, 118-126.

Cunningham, J.B. and Lischeron, J. (1991) Defining Entrepreneurship. Journal of Small Business Management, 29, 45-61.

Cope, J., & Watts, G. (2000). Learning by doing- An exploration of experience, critical incidents and reflection in entrepreneurial learning. *International Journal of Entrepreneurial Behavior & Research, 6(3), 104-124. doi: 10.1108/13552550010346208*

Dalley, J., & Hamilton, B. (2000). Knowledge, Context and Learning in the Small Business. International Small Business Journal, 18(3), 51

Drucker, P. 2007. Innovation and Entrepreneurship. *The Classic Drucker Collection*

Ely, Adams Lorenz & Young, (1917). Outlines of Economics, revised edition (New York: Macmillan)

Fayolle, A. (2007) Entrepreneurship and New Value Creation: The Dynamic of the Entrepreneurial Process. Cambridge University Press, Cambridge.

Fillion. L. J. (2011). Defending the entrepreneur. *World Encyclopaedia of Entrepreneurship*

Gupta, A.L., Smith, K. G., & Shalley, C.E. (2006). The Interplay between Exploration and Exploitation. *The Academy of Management Journal, 49(4), 693-706. Doi: 10.2307/20159793*

Kets De Vries, M.F.R (1977).The Entrepreneurial Personality: A Person At The Crossroads *Journal of Management Studies, Wiley Blackwell*

Kets De Vries, M.F.R (1985). The Dark Side of Entrepreneurship. *Harvard Business Review*

Leibenstein, H. (1968). Entrepreneurship and Development. *American Economic Review*, 58(2), 71.

Longenecker, J. G., & Schoen, J. E. (1975). An empirical investigation of pre-entry socialization of successors for leadership in family-controlled businesses. Paper presented at Management Perspectives on Organizational Effectiveness, Southern Management Association Meetings

Lynn, R. (1969). An Achievement Motivation Questionnaire. *British Journal of Psychology 60, 4.*

Pamler, M. (1971). The Application of Psychological Testing to Entrepreneurial Potential. *California Management Review 13, 31.*

Shane, S., & Venkataraman, S. (2000). The promise of entrepreneurship as a field of research. *The Academy of Management Review, 25*(1), 217–226. https://doi.org/10.2307/259271

Spinelli, S. & Adams, R. (2010). New Venture Creation: Entrepreneurship for the 21st Century. *McGraw-Hill Ryerson Higher Education*

Stevenson H.H. & Gumpert D.E. (1965). Serious

analysis of the sources of opportunity. *The Heart of Entrepreneurship.* Harvard Business Review

Weber, M. (1964). The theory of social and economic organization. New York: The Free Press.

Wilken, P. H (1979). Entrepreneurship. A Comparative and Historic Study.

Womack, J. P., & Jones, D. T. (1996). Lean Thinking: Banish Waste and Create Wealth in Your Corporation. London: Simon & Schuster.

Zaleznik, A. and Kets de Vries, M.F.R. (1976). "What makes entrepreneurs entrepreneurial? *Business and Society Review, Spring, 17.*

Printed in Great Britain
by Amazon

25295421R00073